Sweater Weather

Eight Cozy Chill-in-the-Air Quilts

Susan Ache

Martingale®
Create with Confidence

Sweater Weather: Eight Cozy Chill-in-the-Air Quilts
© 2020 by Susan Ache

Martingale®
19021 120th Ave. NE, Ste. 102
Bothell, WA 98011-9511 USA
ShopMartingale.com

Printed in Hong Kong
25 24 23 22 21 20   8 7 6 5 4 3 2 1

Library of Congress Cataloging-in-Publication Data is available upon request

ISBN: 978-1-68356-064-7

MISSION STATEMENT

We empower makers who use fabric and yarn to make life more enjoyable.

CREDITS

PUBLISHER AND
CHIEF VISIONARY OFFICER
Jennifer Erbe Keltner

CONTENT DIRECTOR
Karen Costello Soltys

DESIGN MANAGER
Adrienne Smitke

MANAGING EDITOR
Tina Cook

PRODUCTION MANAGER
Regina Girard

ACQUISITIONS AND
DEVELOPMENT EDITOR
Laurie Baker

COVER AND
BOOK DESIGNER
Mia Mar

TECHNICAL EDITOR
Elizabeth Beese

PHOTOGRAPHER
Brent Kane

COPY EDITOR
Melissa Bryan

ILLUSTRATOR
Sandy Loi

SPECIAL THANKS
Photography for this book was taken at the home of Kirsten Yanasak in Everett, Washington, and at Lori Clark's the Farmhouse Cottage in Snohomish, Washington.

Thanks go to my wonderful long-arm machine quilter, Susan Rogers.

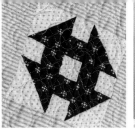

Contents

An Autumn State of Mind

In my perfect fall world, I live on Pumpkin Lane in a big white farmhouse with a red barn and I host weekend bonfire parties. I picture the guests snuggled in cute fall sweaters, wrapped in cozy quilts, sitting on hay bales and watching movies shown on the side of my barn, while I keep the apple cider flowing and the goodie table crowded with treats.

The reality is that I live in Florida and the fall of my daydreams doesn't exist here—our extreme heat lasts well into the autumn season. Does that stop me from making fall-inspired quilts? No way! I just tone down my color palette a bit so it isn't as bright, and then fall quilts can live happily in my sunny house.

Halloween is one of my very favorite holidays to create quilts for. There's just something about a black-and-orange color palette that appeals to me. When I use crisp white fabrics with little black prints as background fabric, I can count on them to always work perfectly with any shade of orange or black, just like a match made in heaven.

If orange-and-black isn't your favorite color scheme, take a visit to your local grocery store. The produce department is one of my favorite places for color inspiration. In the fall, you can't beat the colors of the gourds, vegetables, and fruits that are stacked on the display tables. Next time you go to the market, grab a variety of these fall fruits and veggies and when you get home, take them straight to your sewing room. Play with your fruit and vegetables the way you do your fabric stash—mix and match and come up with your own fall color palette.

While we may not all live in an area that has sweater weather during the fall months, we certainly can create cozy fall decor at home with quilts as the main attraction. Make your own kind of sweater weather, even if you don't have chilling temperatures in your neck of the woods. Embrace the colors of change, even if you don't have the seasons of changing colors. And heck, buy that cute fall sweater, even if you wear it in the air conditioning!

Happy sweater weather!

Susan

Skipping Stones

I have so many fun memories from my childhood. One is of spitting watermelon seeds. (I was a clear winner all the time with that one.) The other is of skipping stones (not so much with that). I always found the rocks that just plopped to the bottom of the stream. But with the right shades of stone fabric against the perfect pond blue, I made a winning "skipping stones" quilt. This quilt was actually designed from the border inward, because I wanted the ripple stone effect. I used short strip sets in order to move the gray stone colors around better and achieve a much scrappier look.

materials

Yardage is based on 42"-wide fabric. Fat quarters are 18" × 21".

- 13 fat quarters of assorted gray prints for blocks and outer border
- 1¼ yards of white solid for blocks
- 1¾ yards of blue print for blocks, sashing squares, borders, and binding
- ⅝ yard of gray dot for sashing and inner border
- 3⅛ yards of fabric for backing
- 55" × 55" piece of batting

cutting

All measurements include ¼" seam allowances.

From *each* gray print fat quarter, cut:

1 strip, 3½" × 21"; crosscut into:
- 1 square, 3½" × 3½" (13 total). Cut each square into quarters diagonally to yield 4 large triangles (52 total; 2 are extra).
- 4 squares, 2" × 2" (52 total). Cut each square in half diagonally to yield 8 small triangles (104 total; 4 are extra).

4 strips, 1½" × 21"; crosscut into:
- 3 strips, 1½" × 9½" (39 total; 2 are extra)
- 8 rectangles, 1½" × 2½" (104 total)
- 16 squares, 1½" × 1½" (208 total; 8 are extra)

From remaining gray print scraps, cut *a total of*:

4 squares, 2½" × 2½"

From the white solid, cut:

2 strips, 3½" × 42"; crosscut into 13 squares, 3½" × 3½". Cut each square into quarters diagonally to yield 52 large triangles (2 are extra).

3 strips, 2" × 42"; crosscut into 50 squares, 2" × 2". Cut each square in half diagonally to yield 100 small triangles.

16 strips, 1½" × 42"; crosscut into:
- 136 rectangles, 1½" × 2½"
- 164 squares, 1½" × 1½"

From the blue print, cut:

4 strips, 3½" × 42"; crosscut into:
- 8 rectangles, 3½" × 6½"
- 28 squares, 3½" × 3½"

10 strips, 2½" × 42"; crosscut 4 of the strips into:
- 7 strips, 2½" × 9½"
- 20 squares, 2½" × 2½"
- 20 rectangles, 1½" × 2½"

11 strips, 1½" × 42"; crosscut into:
- 30 strips, 1½" × 9½"
- 84 squares, 1½" × 1½"

From the gray dot, cut:

11 strips, 1½" × 42"; crosscut into:
- 4 strips, 1½" × 34½"
- 40 strips, 1½" × 6½"

making the squash blossom blocks

To create the nine-patch effect around each sashing square as in the featured quilt on page 9, the outer rows of each Squash Blossom block are not added until the quilt center is being assembled. Press the seam allowances as indicated by the arrows.

1 Use a pencil to mark a diagonal line on the wrong side of each gray 1½" square.

2 Position a marked gray square, right side down, on one end of a white 1½" × 2½" rectangle as shown. Sew on the drawn line. Trim the seam allowances to ¼" and press the resulting triangle open. Add a matching marked square to the opposite end of the white rectangle to make a flying-geese unit measuring 1½" × 2½", including seam allowances. Repeat to make 100 flying-geese units total (25 sets of four matching units).

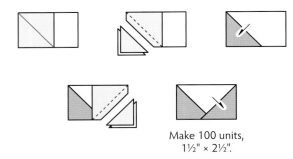

Make 100 units,
1½" × 2½".

3 Sew together small gray and white triangles to make a half-square-triangle unit. Trim to measure 1½" square, including seam allowances. Repeat to make 100 half-square-triangle units (25 sets of four matching units).

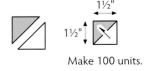

Make 100 units.

4 Lay out two matching gray large triangles and two white large triangles in two pairs as shown. Sew together the triangles in each pair. Join the pairs to make an hourglass unit. Center and trim the hourglass unit to measure 2½" square, including seam allowances. Make 25 hourglass units.

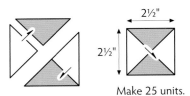

Make 25 units.

5 Matching the gray print in all pieces and units, arrange four white 1½" squares, two flying-geese units, four half-square-triangle units, four gray 1½" × 2½" rectangles, and one hourglass unit in five horizontal rows. Sew the pieces together in each row. Join the rows to make a block unit that measures 4½" × 6½", including seam allowances. Make 25 block units total. (You should have 50 flying-geese units left—two to match each of the 25 block units.)

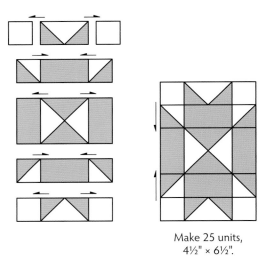

Make 25 units,
4½" × 6½".

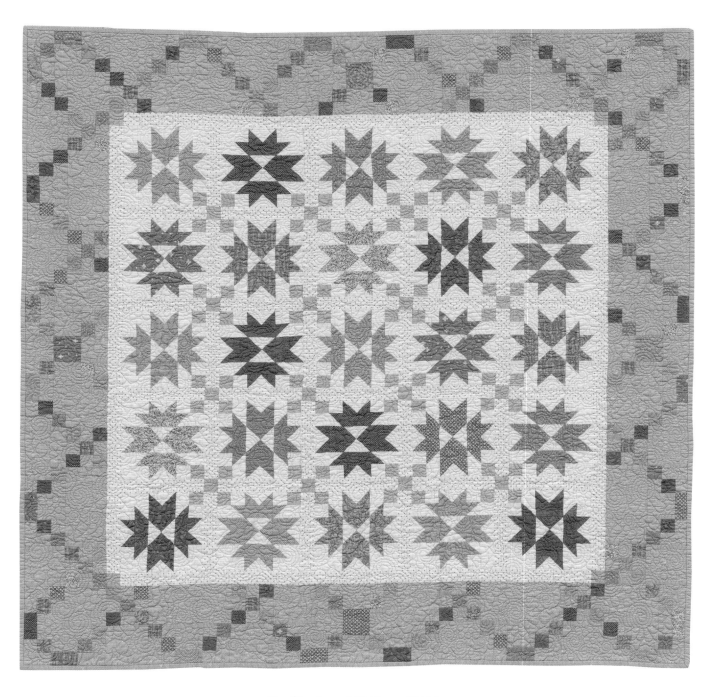

Quilt size: 48½" × 48½"
Block size: 6" × 6"

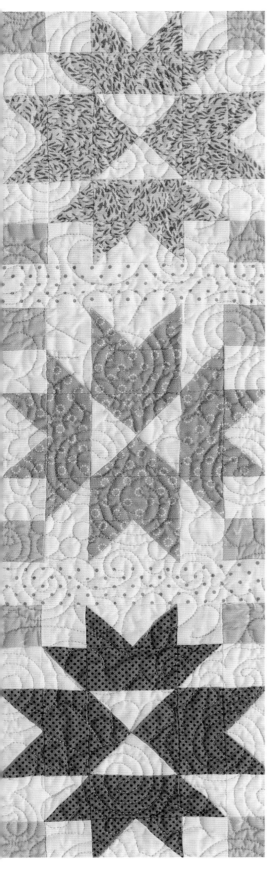

assembling the quilt top

1 Referring to the quilt center layout diagram, arrange the block units, gray dot 1½" × 6½" sashing strips, and 16 blue 1½" sashing squares in nine rows on your design wall; rotate every other block unit as shown. To create the nine-patch effect around each sashing square, you will add blue 1½" squares in different positions to the blocks. Label each block A, B, C, D, or E as shown in the layout.

Quilt center layout

2 To complete block A, remove an A block unit from your design wall and position the following pieces in columns on either side of the block: three white 1½" × 2½" rectangles, the two flying-geese units that match the block unit, one white 1½" square, and one blue 1½" square. Sew the pieces together in each column. Add the columns to the block unit to make block A, which should measure 6½" square, including seam allowances. Make two A blocks and return them to the design wall after piecing to prevent confusion when assembling the quilt top.

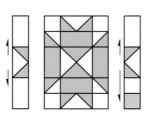 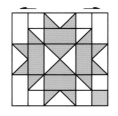

Block A.
Make 2 blocks,
6½" × 6½".

3 Position the following pieces in columns on either side of a B block unit: three white 1½" × 2½" rectangles, the two flying-geese units that match the block unit, one white 1½" square, and one blue 1½" square. Sew the pieces together in each column. Add the columns to the block unit to make block B, which should measure 6½" square, including seam allowances. Make two B blocks.

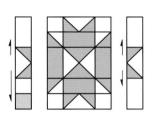
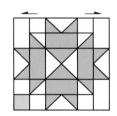

Block B.
Make 2 blocks,
6½" × 6½".

5 Position the following pieces in columns on either side of a D block unit: two white 1½" × 2½" rectangles, the two flying-geese units that match the block unit, two white 1½" squares, and two blue 1½" squares. Sew the pieces together in each column. Add the columns to the block unit to make block D, which should measure 6½" square, including seam allowances. Make six D blocks.

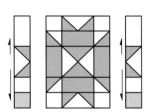
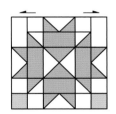

Block D.
Make 6 blocks,
6½" × 6½".

4 Position the following pieces in columns on either side of a C block unit: two blue 1½" squares, two white 1½" squares, the two flying-geese units that match the block unit, and two white 1½" × 2½" rectangles. Sew the pieces together in each column. Add the columns to the block unit to make block C, which should measure 6½" square, including seam allowances. Make six C blocks.

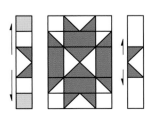
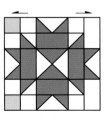

Block C.
Make 6 blocks,
6½" × 6½".

6 Position the following pieces in columns on either side of an E block unit: four blue 1½" squares, four white 1½" squares, and the two flying-geese units that match the block unit. Sew the pieces together in each column. Add the columns to the block unit to make block E, which should measure 6½" square, including seam allowances. Make nine E blocks.

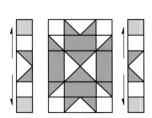
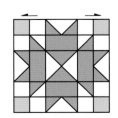

Block E.
Make 9 blocks,
6½" × 6½".

7 Once all the blocks are complete, sew together the pieces in each row as shown in the quilt assembly diagram below. Join the rows to make the quilt center, which should measure 34½" square, including seam allowances.

> ### Susan says . . .
>
> *Because of all of the variety of pieces in this quilt, it works best to use clear sandwich bags to keep yourself organized as you sew all of the different parts together. Label each bag clearly by the size of piece or the name of the segment it contains.*

making border units

1 Sew together blue and gray 1½" × 9½" strips in pairs to make 12 of strip set A. Crosscut the strip sets into 48 A1 segments, 1½" wide, and 12 A2 segments, 2½" wide.

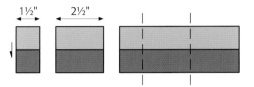

Make 12 of strip set A, 2½" × 9½".
Cut 48 A1 segments, 1½" × 2½".
Cut 12 A2 segments, 2½" × 2½".

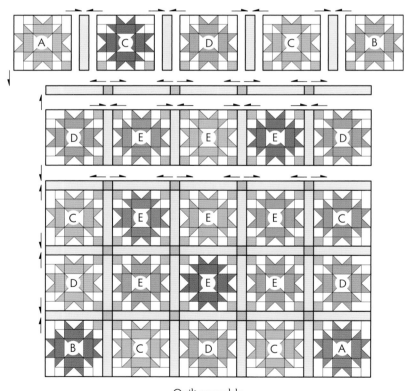

Quilt assembly

2 Join blue 2½" × 9½" strips and gray 1½" × 9½" strips in pairs to make seven of strip set B. Crosscut the strip sets into 28 B1 segments, 1½" wide, and eight B2 segments, 2½" wide.

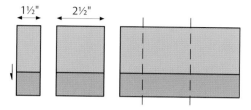

Make 7 of strip set B, 3½" × 9½".
Cut 28 B1 segments, 1½" × 3½".
Cut 8 B2 segments, 2½" × 3½".

3 Sew together one gray and two blue 1½" × 9½" strips to make strip set C. Make six. Crosscut the strip sets into 32 C segments, 1½" wide.

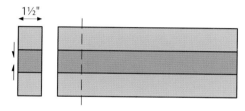

Make 6 of strip set C, 3½" × 9½".
Cut 32 C segments, 1½" × 3½".

4 Join one blue and two assorted gray 1½" × 9½" strips to make strip set D. Make six. Crosscut the strip sets into 32 D segments, 1½" wide.

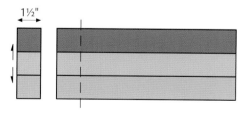

Make 6 of strip set D, 3½" × 9½".
Cut 32 D segments, 1½" × 3½".

5 Join two A1 segments to make a four-patch unit that measures 2½" square, including seam allowances. Make 12 four-patch units.

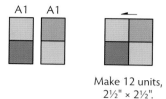

Make 12 units,
2½" × 2½".

6 Join two D segments and one C segment to make a nine-patch unit that measures 3½" square, including seam allowances. Make 16 nine-patch units.

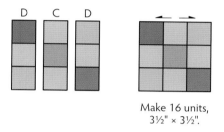

Make 16 units,
3½" × 3½".

adding the borders

1 Lay out the following pieces in two horizontal rows: two blue 3½" squares, two B1 segments, two C segments, and one B2 segment in the top row, and two nine-patch units and one blue 3½" × 6½" rectangle in the bottom row. Sew together the pieces in each row. Join the rows to make border unit 1, which should measure 6½" × 12½", including seam allowances. Make eight of border unit 1.

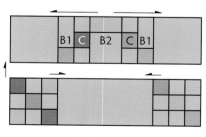

Border unit 1.
Make 8 units,
6½" × 12½".

2 Lay out the following pieces in two horizontal rows. Top row: two blue 1½" × 2½" rectangles, four A1 segments, two A2 segments, and one blue 2½" square. Bottom row: two B1 segments, two blue 3½" squares, three blue 2½" squares, two four-patch units, and one gray 2½" square. Join each piece in the columns of the bottom horizontal row. Then sew the units or pieces together in each row. Join the rows to make border unit 2, which should measure 6½" × 12½", including seam allowances. Make four of border unit 2.

3 Lay out the following pieces in two columns. Left column: two blue 1½" × 2½" rectangles, two A1 segments, and one A2 segment. Right column: one gray 1½" × 2½" rectangle, one blue 1½" × 2½" rectangle, one blue 2½" square, one four-patch unit, one B1 segment, and one blue 3½" square. Join pieces in horizontal pairs as shown. Then sew together the pieces in each column. Join the columns to make border unit 3, which should measure 6½" square, including seam allowances. Make four of border unit 3.

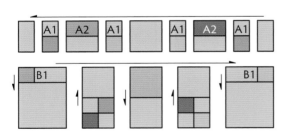

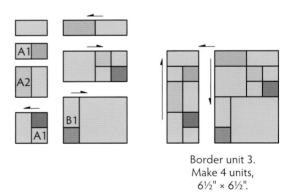

Border unit 3.
Make 4 units,
6½" × 6½".

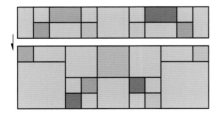

Border unit 2.
Make 4 units,
6½" × 12½".

4 Lay out two of border unit 1 and one of border unit 2 in a row as shown. Sew the units together to make a short outer-border row that measures 6½" × 36½", including seam allowances. Make four rows.

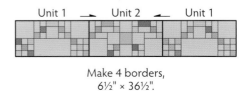

Make 4 borders,
6½" × 36½".

5 Noting the rotation of the border units, add a border unit 3 to each end of two rows from step 4 to make two long outer-border rows. Each row should measure 6½" × 48½", including seam allowances.

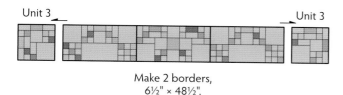

Unit 3   Unit 3

Make 2 borders,
6½" × 48½".

6 For the inner border, sew gray dot 1½" × 34½" strips to opposite edges of the quilt top. Sew blue 1½" squares to each end of the remaining gray dot strips, and sew these strips to the remaining edges of the quilt top. The quilt top should measure 36½" square, including seam allowances.

7 Sew the short outer-border rows to opposite edges of the quilt top. Add the long outer-border rows to the remaining edges to complete the quilt top.

finishing the quilt

Find free, detailed finishing instructions online at ShopMartingale.com/HowtoQuilt.

1 Prepare the quilt backing so that it is about 4" larger in both directions than the quilt top.

2 Layer the backing, right side down; the batting; and the quilt top, right side up. Baste the layers together.

3 Hand or machine quilt as desired. The quilt shown is machine quilted with an allover design of spirals interspersed with feathers and pebbles.

4 Using the blue 2½"-wide strips, make the binding and attach it to the quilt.

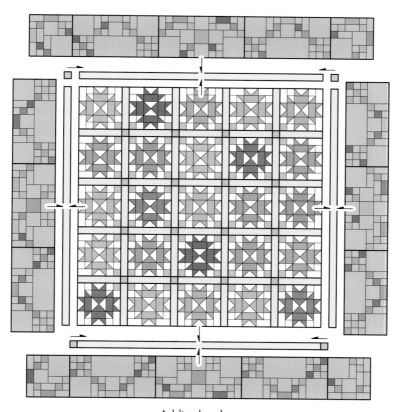

Adding borders

Halloween-ish

The combination of white and black can make a bold statement, or it can create a subtle background as shown here. I had been setting aside my white-and-black prints for weeks without a plan in place, knowing that I wanted them all to be together in something, and also knowing I wanted to use them as rather large focal points instead of cutting them into small pieces. Halloween-ish just happened when I put a piece of orange fabric on top of the stack. What better way to show how cute the prints themselves are, than by adding a hint of color? You could make this quilt for every season using every sort of low-volume print available. It's such a fun "collecting" kind of quilt to bring together your perfect mix of fabrics.

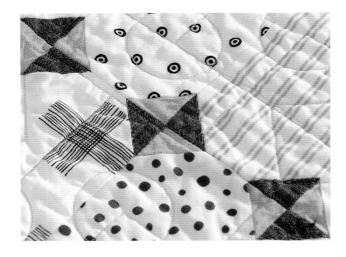

materials

Yardage is based on 42"-wide fabric. Fat quarters are 18" × 21".

- 20 or more fat quarters of assorted white-and-black prints (collectively referred to as "white") for blocks*
- ⅞ yard of black print for blocks
- ⅞ yard of orange print for blocks
- ⅝ yard of off-white solid for binding
- 3⅝ yards of fabric for backing
- 64" × 79" piece of batting

The featured quilt was constructed using 34 fat quarters for lots of variety.

cutting

All measurements include ¼" seam allowances.

From the assorted white prints, cut:
78 strips, 3½" × 21"; crosscut into:
- 209 rectangles, 3½" × 6½"
- 38 squares, 3½" × 3½"

From the black print, cut:
17 strips, 1½" × 42"; crosscut into 432 squares, 1½" × 1½"

From the orange print, cut:
17 strips, 1½" × 42"; crosscut into 432 squares, 1½" × 1½"

From the off-white solid, cut:
7 strips, 2½" × 42"

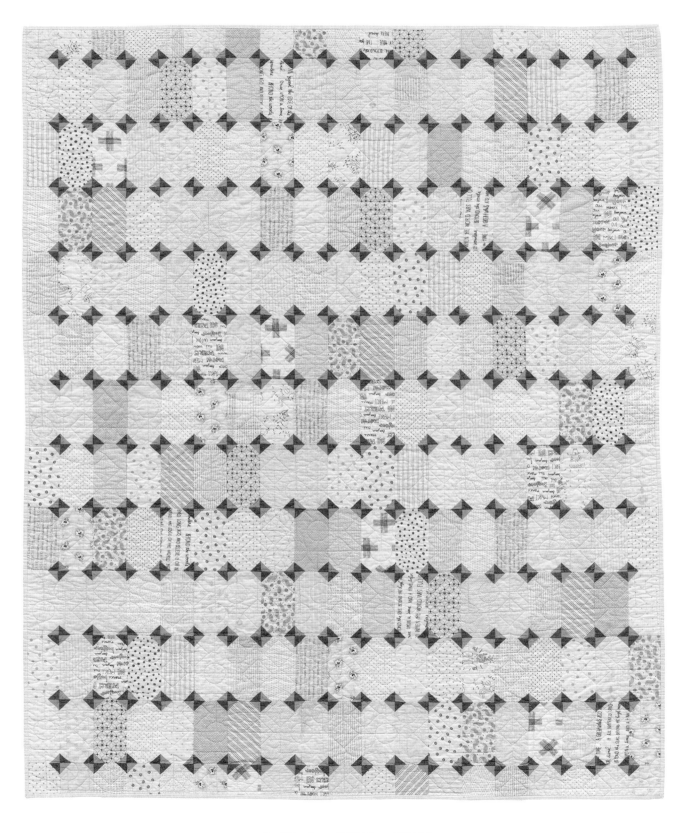

Quilt size: 57½" × 72½"
Block size: 3" × 6"

making the blocks and border units

Press the seam allowances as indicated by the arrows.

1 Use a pencil to mark a diagonal line on the wrong side of each black and orange 1½" square.

2 Align a marked black square, right sides together, on each corner of a white 3½" × 6½" rectangle. Sew on the drawn lines. Trim the seam allowances to ¼" and press the resulting triangle toward the corner to make a black block that measures 3½" × 6½", including seam allowances. Make 94 black blocks.

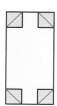 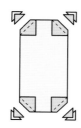 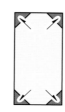

Make 94 blocks,
3½" × 6½".

3 In the same manner, sew four marked orange squares to a white 3½" × 6½" rectangle to make an orange block; note that the seam allowances are pressed in the opposite direction as the black blocks. Make 93 orange blocks.

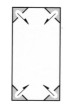

Make 93 blocks,
3½" × 6½".

4 Using the same method as before, add two marked black squares to a white 3½" × 6½" rectangle as shown to make a black A border unit. Make 10 units. Using marked orange squares and pressing in the opposite direction, make 12 orange A border units.

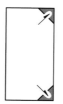 

Black A unit.
Make 10 units,
3½" × 6½".

Orange A unit.
Make 12 units,
3½" × 6½".

5 In the same manner, add two marked black squares to a white 3½" square as shown to make a black B border unit. Make 16 units. Using marked orange squares and pressing in the opposite direction, make 18 orange B border units.

Black B unit.
Make 16 units,
3½" × 3½".

Orange B unit.
Make 18 units,
3½" × 3½".

6 Using the same method, add one marked black square to a white 3½" square as shown to make a black C border unit. Make four units.

C unit.
Make 4 units,
3½" × 3½".

2 Sew together the pieces in each row. Join the rows to complete the quilt top.

finishing the quilt

Find free, detailed finishing instructions online at ShopMartingale.com/HowtoQuilt.

1 Prepare the quilt backing so that it is about 6" larger in both directions than the quilt top.

2 Layer the backing, right side down; the batting; and the quilt top, right side up. Baste the layers together.

3 Hand or machine quilt as desired. The quilt shown is machine quilted with an allover geometric design of circles and squares connected by straight lines.

4 Using the off-white solid 2½"-wide strips, make the binding and attach it to the quilt.

assembling the quilt top

Instead of piecing the blocks and borders separately, I joined all the pieces in 13 horizontal rows. This leaves less room for error than piecing the side borders first and then attaching them to the quilt center.

1 Referring to the quilt assembly diagram below, lay out the blocks and border units in 13 rows. Make sure that all blocks and units alternate between black corners and orange corners.

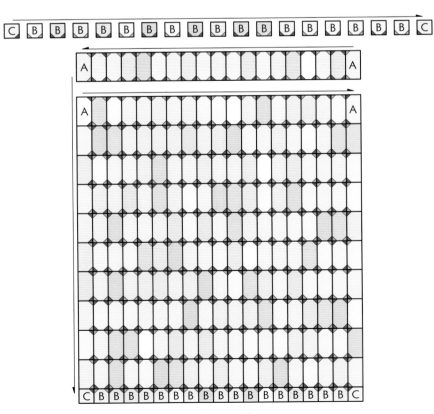

Quilt assembly

Starburst

Who wouldn't love the chance to make a Lone Star quilt with all of the fun but none of the Y-seams? I can honestly say that a Lone Star with no Y-seams is just about my favorite block to make—so many pretty combinations are possible, and there are so many seasons to hunt for fabric. I specifically chose Halloween colors for our annual family shindig, just big enough to drape off the end of my buffet table for added pizzazz.

materials

Yardage is based on 42"-wide fabric.

- ¼ yard of white-and-orange dot for center block
- ½ yard of black dot for center block and borders 1–3
- ¼ yard of orange brocade for center block and border 1
- ⅛ yard of orange check for center block
- ¼ yard of white print for center block background
- 11 strips, 2½" × 42", of assorted orange prints for border 2
- 11 strips, 2½" × 42", of assorted white prints for border 2
- 1 yard of white dot for borders 2 and 4
- ½ yard of orange floral for binding
- 2½ yards of fabric for backing*
- 45" × 45" piece of batting
- Acrylic ruler with 45° line

*If your fabric is at least 45" wide, you will need only 1¼ yards.

cutting

All measurements include ¼" seam allowances.

From the white-and-orange dot, cut:
2 strips, 2" × 42"; crosscut *1 of the strips* into 2 strips, 2" × 21"

From the black dot, cut:
1 strip, 2¼" × 42"; crosscut into 12 squares, 2¼" × 2¼"

1 strip, 2" × 21"

7 strips, 1½" × 42"; crosscut into:
- 2 strips, 1½" × 35"
- 2 strips, 1½" × 33"
- 8 strips, 1½" × 11"

From the orange brocade, cut:
2 strips, 2¼" × 42"; crosscut into 8 strips, 2¼" × 7¾"

1 strip, 2" × 42"; crosscut into 2 strips, 2" × 21" (1 is extra)

From the orange check, cut:
1 strip, 2" × 42"

Continued on page 23

Continued from page 21

From the white print, cut:

1 strip, 5⅛" × 42"; crosscut into:
- 4 squares, 5⅛" × 5⅛"; cut each square in half diagonally to yield 8 large triangles
- 4 squares, 3⅞" × 3⅞"; cut each square in half diagonally to yield 8 small triangles

From *each* orange print strip, cut:

1 strip, 1½" × 42"; crosscut into 3 strips, 1½" × 11" (33 total; 1 is extra)

From *each* white print strip, cut:

1 strip, 1½" × 42"; crosscut into 3 strips, 1½" × 11" (33 total; 1 is extra)

From the white dot, cut:

1 strip, 5⅛" × 42"; crosscut into 4 squares, 5⅛" × 5⅛". Cut each square in half diagonally to yield 8 large triangles.

3 strips, 3⅞" × 42"; crosscut into 28 squares, 3⅞" × 3⅞". Cut each square in half diagonally to yield 56 small triangles.

4 strips, 3½" × 42"; crosscut into:
- 2 strips, 3½" × 41"
- 2 strips, 3½" × 35"

From the orange floral, cut:

5 strips, 2½" × 42"

making the center block

Press the seam allowances as indicated by the arrows.

1 Sew together a white-and-orange dot 2" × 21" strip and the black dot 2" × 21" strip to make strip set A. Using a rotary cutter, mat, and the 45° line on an acrylic ruler, trim one end of the strip set at a 45° angle. Rotate the strip set so that the cut edge is on the left. Cutting parallel to the trimmed edge, cut four A segments, 2" wide.

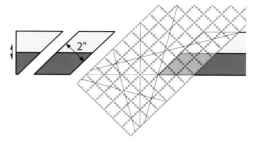

Make 1 strip set, 3½" × 21".
Cut 4 A segments, 2" wide.

Susan says . . .

Piecing 45° angles may seem intimidating at first, but my best advice is to press the seam allowances in the strip sets open. This helps the fabric lie completely flat when you are pressing the rest of the block. Truly, once you make a few strip sets, you will get your sewing rhythm going and see that the seam allowances fall perfectly in place.

2 Sew together a white-and-orange dot 2" × 42" strip and the orange check 2" × 42" strip to make strip set B. In the same manner as in step 1, trim one end at a 45° angle and cut eight B segments, 2" wide.

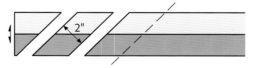

Make 1 strip set, 3½" × 42".
Cut 8 B segments, 2" wide.

Quilt size: 41" × 41"
Center block size: 14½" × 14½"

3 Sew together the white-and-orange dot 2" × 21" strip and the orange brocade 2" × 21" strip to make strip set C. In the same manner as in step 1, trim one end at a 45° angle and cut four C segments, 2" wide.

Make 1 strip set, 3½" × 21".
Cut 4 C segments, 2" wide.

4 Lay out one A and one B segment as shown. Place the segments right sides together and insert a pin into the seam ¼" from the edge of one segment; poke the pin through the second segment in the same manner to align the center seams. Sew together to make a black-tip diamond. Make four.

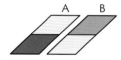

Make 4 units.

5 In the same manner as in step 4, join one B segment and one C segment to make an orange-tip diamond. Make four.

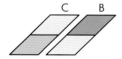
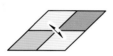

Make 4 units.

6 Sew a white print small triangle to the orange-check edge of an orange-tip diamond as shown. Add a white print large triangle to the opposite edge to make a star-point unit. Repeat to make four matching orange star-point units.

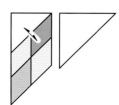
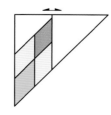

Make 4 orange star-point units.

7 Paying close attention to orientation and using a black-tip diamond, add white print small and large triangles to the orange-check edge of the diamond to make a black star-point unit. Make four matching units.

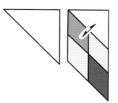
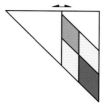

Make 4 black star-point units.

8 Sew together an orange star-point unit and a black star-point unit to make a quarter block that measures 7¾" square, including seam allowances. Repeat to make four matching quarter blocks.

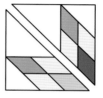
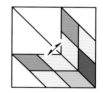

Make 4 quarter blocks,
7¾" × 7¾".

9 Lay out the quarter blocks in two rows of two. Sew the quarter blocks into rows, and then join the rows to make the center block. The center block should measure 15" square, including seam allowances.

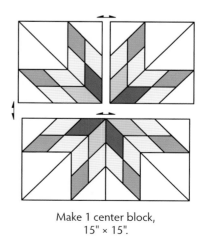

Make 1 center block,
15" × 15".

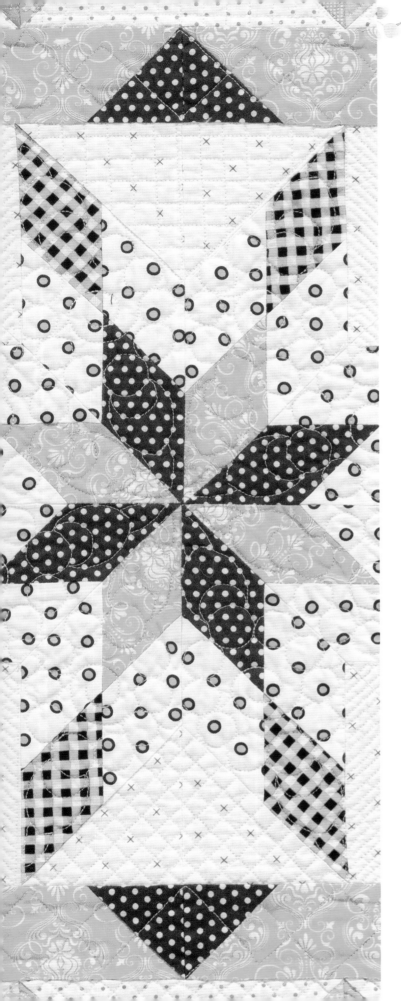

assembling border 1

1 Use a pencil to mark a diagonal line on the wrong side of eight black dot 2¼" squares.

2 Position a marked square, right side down, on one end of an orange brocade 2¼" × 7¾" strip. Sew on the drawn line. Trim the seam allowances to ¼" and press the resulting triangle open to make an inner-border unit. Make four units.

Make 4 units,
2¼" × 7¾".

3 In the same manner, add a marked square to the opposite end of an orange brocade 2¼" × 7¾" strip as shown to make a mirror-image inner-border unit. Make four units.

Make 4 units,
2¼" × 7¾".

4 Sew together an inner-border unit and a mirror-image inner-border unit to make a short border 1 strip. The strip should measure 2¼" × 15", including seam allowances. Make four.

Make 4 borders,
2¼" × 15".

5 Add a remaining black dot 2¼" square to each end of a strip from step 4. Make two long border 1 strips that measure 2¼" × 18½", including seam allowances.

Make 2 borders,
2¼" × 18½".

assembling border 2

1 Offsetting the ends by 1" as shown, sew together two different orange print 1½" × 11" strips and one white print 1½" × 11" strip to make strip set D. Make 16 of strip set D. In the same manner as for the center block, trim one end of each strip set at a 45° angle. Cutting parallel to the trimmed edge, cut four D segments, 1½" wide, from each strip set (64 total).

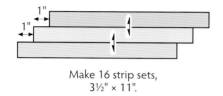

Make 16 strip sets, 3½" × 11".

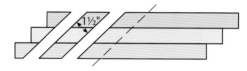

Cut 64 D segments, 1½" wide.

2 Offsetting the ends by 1", join two different white print 1½" × 11" strips and one black dot 1½" × 11" strip to make strip set E. Make eight of strip set E. Trim one end of each strip set at a 45° angle and cut four E segments, 1½" wide, from each strip set (32 total).

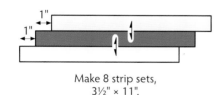

Make 8 strip sets, 3½" × 11".

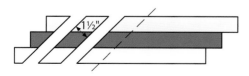

Cut 32 E segments, 1½" wide.

3 Using pins to align seams as when making the center block diamonds, join two D segments and one E segment as shown to make a border diamond. Make 32 border diamonds.

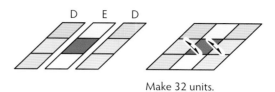

Make 32 units.

4 In the same manner as for the center block, add a white dot large triangle and a white dot small triangle to adjacent edges of a border diamond as shown to make a star-point unit. Make four. Adding the triangles to the opposite edges of the border diamond, repeat to make four mirror-image star-point units.

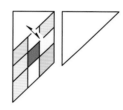
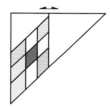

Make 4 star-point units.

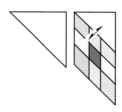
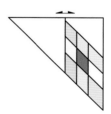

Make 4 star-point units.

5 Sew together a star-point unit and a mirror-image star-point unit to make a quarter block. The quarter block should measure 7¾" square, including seam allowances. Repeat to make four matching quarter blocks.

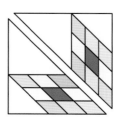
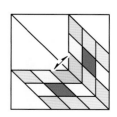

Make 4 quarter blocks, 7¾" × 7¾".

6 Sew two white dot small triangles to opposite edges of a remaining border diamond as shown to make a border unit. Make 12. Adding small triangles as shown, make 12 mirror-image border units.

 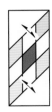 

Make 12 of each unit,
3½" × 7¾".

7 Sew together three border units and three mirror-image border units in a row as shown to make a short border 2. The border should be 7¾" × 18½", including seam allowances. Make four short border 2 strips.

  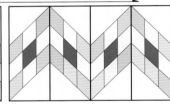

Make 4 borders,
7¾" × 18½".

8 Sew a quarter block to each end of a short border 2 strip. Make two long border 2 strips measuring 7¾" × 33", including seam allowances.

 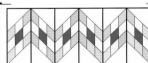

Make 2 borders,
7¾" × 33".

assembling the quilt top

1 Sew the short border 1 strips to opposite edges of the center block. Add the long border 1 strips to the remaining edges. The quilt top should measure 18½" square, including seam allowances.

2 Sew the short border 2 strips to opposite edges of the quilt top. Add the long border 2 strips to the remaining edges. The quilt top should measure 33" square, including seam allowances.

3 Sew the black dot 1½" × 33" strips to opposite edges of the quilt top. Add the black dot 1½" × 35" strips to the remaining edges. The quilt top should measure 35" square, including seam allowances.

4 Sew the white dot 3½" × 35" strips to opposite edges of the quilt top. Add the white dot 3½" × 41" strips to the remaining edges to complete the quilt top.

finishing the quilt

Find free, detailed finishing instructions online at ShopMartingale.com/HowtoQuilt.

1 Prepare the quilt backing so that it is about 4" larger in both directions than the quilt top.

2 Layer the backing, right side down; the batting; and the quilt top, right side up. Baste the layers together.

3 Hand or machine quilt as desired. The center of the quilt shown is machine quilted with a spiral design in the star, fleur-de-lis surrounded by parallel lines in the corners, and a diagonal grid in the white print triangles at the star points. Border 1 is filled with a diamond design. Border 2 has a spiral design filling the border diamonds and a diagonal grid in the white dot triangles. A Baptist Fan design spans borders 3 and 4.

4 Using the orange floral 2½"-wide strips, make the binding and attach it to the quilt.

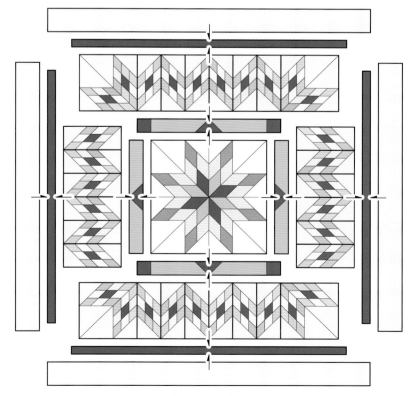

Quilt assembly

Bear Paw Bow Ties

Do bears plan a social before they go into hibernation? If they do, they certainly would look spiffy in some bear ties. How about a fun little alternative to some traditional Bow Tie quilt blocks? Your combination options are endless with this cute tie for such an important event.

materials

Yardage is based on 42"-wide fabric. Fat eighths are 9" × 21".

- 18 fat eighths of assorted medium or dark prints (3 dark blue, 4 light blue, 4 turquoise, 3 dark gray, and 4 gray) for Bear Paw blocks
- 18 fat eighths of assorted shirting prints for Bear Paw blocks and setting squares
- ⅞ yard of taupe print for Double Four Patch blocks, outer border, and binding
- 1¼ yards of white-and-gray polka dot for Double Four Patch blocks, setting triangles, and borders
- 2¾ yards of fabric for backing
- 49" × 49" piece of batting

cutting

All measurements include ¼" seam allowances.

From each medium or dark print, cut:

2 squares, 3½" × 3½" (36 total)

4 squares, 2½" × 2½" (72 total); cut each square in half diagonally to yield 8 triangles (144 total)

4 squares, 2" × 2" (72 total)

From each shirting print, cut:

1 square, 5" × 5" (18 total; 3 are extra)

4 squares, 2½" × 2½" (72 total); cut each square in half diagonally to yield 8 triangles (144 total)

2 squares, 2" × 2" (36 total)

From the taupe print, cut:

10 strips, 2½" × 42"; crosscut *5 of the strips* into:
- 40 rectangles, 2½" × 4½"
- 4 squares, 2½" × 2½"

2 strips, 1⅝" × 42"

From the white-and-gray polka dot, cut:

1 strip, 8" × 42"; crosscut into 4 squares, 8" × 8". Cut each square into quarters diagonally to yield 16 side triangles.

1 strip, 5" × 42"; crosscut into:
- 2 squares, 5" × 5"; cut each square into quarters diagonally to yield 8 small triangles
- 2 squares, 4½" × 4½"; cut each square in half diagonally to yield 4 corner triangles

2 strips, 2¾" × 42"; crosscut into 20 squares, 2¾" × 2¾"

5 strips, 2" × 42"; crosscut into 80 squares, 2" × 2"

2 strips, 1⅝" × 42"

4 strips, 1½" × 42"; crosscut into:
- 2 strips, 1½" × 40½"
- 2 strips, 1½" × 38½"

Quilt size: 44½" × 44½"

Block size: 4½" × 4½"

making the blocks

Press the seam allowances as indicated by the arrows.

1 Sew together a medium or dark triangle and a shirting triangle to make a half-square-triangle unit. Trim the unit to measure 2" square, including seam allowances. Make eight matching half-square-triangle units.

Make 8 units.

2 Matching the fabrics used in step 1, arrange one shirting 2" square, one medium or dark 3½" square, and four half-square-triangle units in two columns as shown. Sew together the half-square-triangle units in each column, and then join the remaining pieces in each column. Sew the columns together to make a Bear Paw block measuring 5" square, including seam allowances. Make a second matching Bear Paw block.

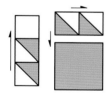

Make 2 blocks,
5" × 5".

3 Repeat steps 1 and 2 to make 36 Bear Paw blocks total (18 pairs of matching blocks).

making the four-patch units

1 Sew together a taupe 1⅝" × 42" strip and a white-and-gray 1⅝" × 42" strip to make a strip set. Make two strip sets. Crosscut the strip sets into 48 segments, 1⅝" wide.

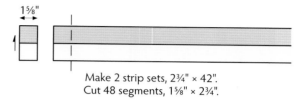

Make 2 strip sets, 2¾" × 42".
Cut 48 segments, 1⅝" × 2¾".

2 Join two segments from step 1 to make a four-patch unit measuring 2¾" square, including seam allowances. Make 24 four-patch units.

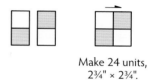

Make 24 units,
2¾" × 2¾".

3 Lay out two four-patch units and two white-and-gray 2¾" squares in two rows as shown. Sew together the pieces in each row. Join the rows to make a Double Four Patch block measuring 5" square, including seam allowances. Make 10 Double Four Patch blocks.

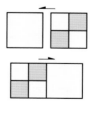 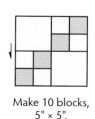

Make 10 blocks,
5" × 5".

4 Sew a white-and-gray small triangle to one edge of a remaining four-patch unit as shown. Add a second white-and-gray small triangle to the adjacent edge to make a four-patch setting triangle. Make four.

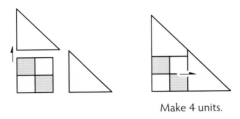

Make 4 units.

assembling the quilt top

1 Use a pencil to mark a diagonal line on the wrong side of each medium or dark 2" square. Sort the marked squares into 18 sets of four marked squares each.

2 Referring to the quilt layout diagram, arrange the Bear Paw blocks, six white-and-gray side triangles, 15 assorted shirting 5" squares, and the Double Four Patch blocks in diagonal rows on your design wall.

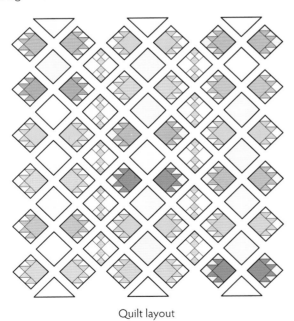

Quilt layout

3 At each point where two matching Bear Paw blocks meet, arrange four matching marked squares, right sides together, on the intersecting pieces as shown; pin in place on the design wall. Using one set of four squares at a time, refer to steps 4–6 that follow to add the marked squares to the Bear Paw blocks, side triangles, and setting squares; return each piece to the design wall after piecing to prevent confusion when assembling the quilt top.

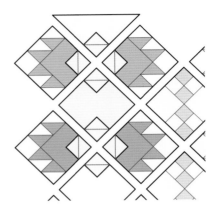

4 To add a marked square to a Bear Paw block, position the square, right side down, on one corner of the block as shown. Sew on the drawn line. Trim the seam allowances to ¼" and press the resulting triangle open; press the seam allowances toward the center of the Bear Paw block.

Make 36 blocks, 5" × 5".

5 To add a marked square to a side triangle, position the square, right side down, on the right-angle corner of the setting triangle as shown. Sew on the drawn line. Trim the seam allowances to ¼" and press the resulting triangle open. Make six pieced setting triangles.

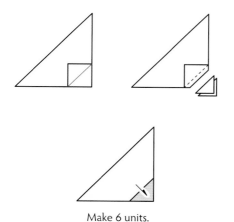

Make 6 units.

6 To add marked squares to a setting square, position the squares, right side down, on opposite corners of the setting square as shown. Sew on the drawn lines. Trim the seam allowances to ¼" and press the resulting triangles open. Make 15 pieced setting squares.

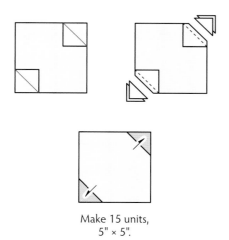

Make 15 units,
5" × 5".

7 Referring to the quilt assembly diagram below, add the remaining white-and-gray side triangles and the four-patch setting triangles to the quilt layout. Note that the setting triangles are oversized and will be trimmed after assembly. Sew together the pieces in each diagonal row.

8 Join the rows and add the corner triangles. Carefully trim the excess from the side and corner triangles, ¼" beyond the points of the blocks. The quilt top should measure 38½" square, including seam allowances.

adding the borders

1 Use a pencil to mark a diagonal line on the wrong side of each white-and-gray 2" square.

2 Position marked squares, right side down, on opposite corners of a taupe 2½" × 4½" rectangle as shown above right. Sew on the drawn lines. Trim

the seam allowances to ¼" and press the resulting triangles open; be sure to press seam allowances in opposite directions as shown to prevent bulk when joining the units. Make 40 border units that each measure 2½" × 4½", including seam allowances.

Make 40 units,
2½" × 4½".

3 Sew together 10 border units to make a strip that measures 2½" × 40½", including seam allowances. Make four short outer-border strips.

Make 4 borders,
2½" × 40½".

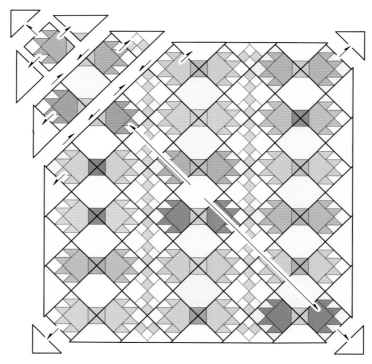

Quilt assembly

4 Add taupe 2½" squares to each end of two strips from step 3 to make two long outer-border strips. Each strip should measure 2½" × 44½", including seam allowances.

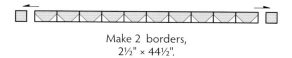

Make 2 borders,
2½" × 44½".

5 For the inner border, sew the white-and-gray 1½" × 38½" strips to opposite edges of the quilt top. Add the white-and-gray 1½" × 40½" strips to the remaining edges. The quilt top should now measure 40½" square, including seam allowances.

6 Sew the short outer-border strips to opposite edges of the quilt top. Add the long outer-border strips to the remaining edges to complete the quilt top.

finishing the quilt

Find free, detailed finishing instructions online at ShopMartingale.com/HowtoQuilt.

1 Prepare the quilt backing so that it is about 6" larger in both directions than the quilt top.

2 Layer the backing, right side down; the batting; and the quilt top, right side up. Baste the layers together.

3 Hand or machine quilt as desired. The quilt shown is machine quilted with pairs of wavy horizontal lines, and between the pairs of lines is a circle-and-square spiral design.

4 Using the taupe 2½"-wide strips, make the binding and attach it to the quilt.

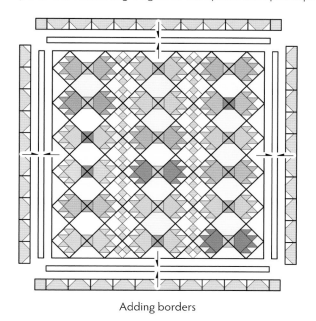

Adding borders

Team Picnic

Count me in for the cheerleading part of anything related to team sports. I love a stadium filled with team colors, and don't even get me started about the wonderful sounds of a marching band. Team Picnic is such a great quilt to make as a special gift for that sports nut in your home. With the great choices of solids out there, I am sure you can come up with your very own team picnic.

materials

Yardage is based on 42"-wide fabric.

- 2 yards of green solid for blocks and binding
- 2½ yards of white print for blocks, setting squares, and setting rectangles
- ¾ yard of navy solid for blocks
- ¾ yard of orange solid for blocks
- 3⅜ yards of fabric for backing
- 60" × 71" piece of batting

cutting

All measurements include ¼" seam allowances.

From the green solid, cut:

7 strips, 2½" × 42"

36 strips, 1¼" × 42"; crosscut *10 of the strips* into 60 rectangles, 1¼" × 5¾"

From the white print, cut:

4 strips, 5¾" × 42"; crosscut into:
- 20 squares, 5¾" × 5¾"
- 8 rectangles, 3½" × 5¾"

2 strips, 3½" × 42"; crosscut into:
- 10 rectangles, 3½" × 5¾"
- 4 squares, 3½" × 3½"

39 strips, 1¼" × 42"

From the navy solid, cut:

18 strips, 1¼" × 42"; crosscut *7 of the strips* into:
- 30 rectangles, 1¼" × 4¼"
- 60 rectangles, 1¼" × 2"

From the orange solid, cut:

18 strips, 1¼" × 42"; crosscut *7 of the strips* into:
- 30 rectangles, 1¼" × 4¼"
- 60 rectangles, 1¼" × 2"

making the blocks

Press the seam allowances as indicated by the arrows.

1 Sew together a green 1¼" × 42" strip and a white 1¼" × 42" strip to make strip set A. Make six. Crosscut the strip sets into 180 A segments, 1¼" wide.

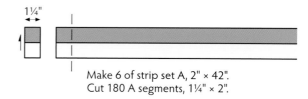

Make 6 of strip set A, 2" × 42".
Cut 180 A segments, 1¼" × 2".

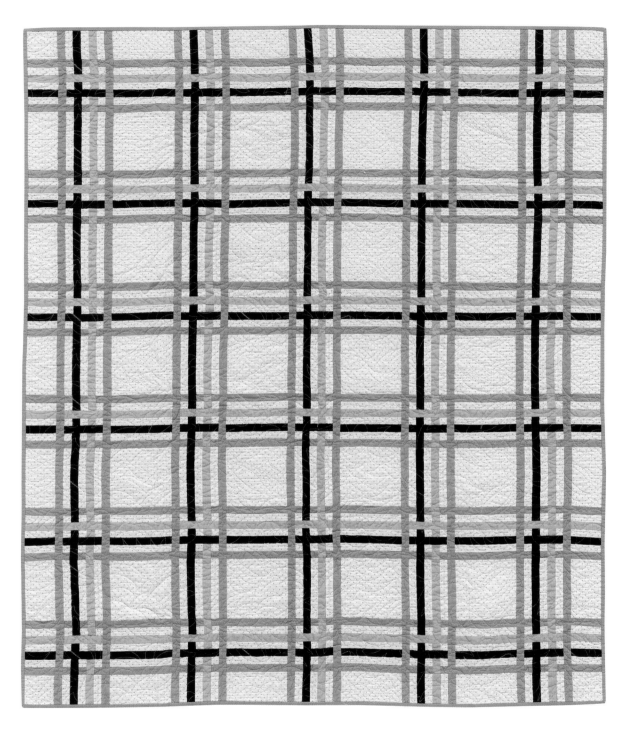

Quilt size: 53¾" × 64¼"
Block size: 5¼" × 5¼"

2 Join one orange, one navy, and three white 1¼" × 42" strips as shown to make strip set B. Crosscut the strip set into 30 B segments, 1¼" wide.

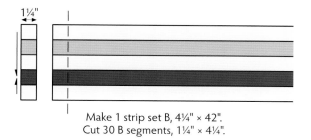

Make 1 strip set B, 4¼" × 42".
Cut 30 B segments, 1¼" × 4¼".

3 Lay out the following pieces in two rows: six A segments, two navy 1¼" x 2" rectangles, and two orange 1¼" x 2" rectangles. Be sure to arrange the A segments as shown, creating mirror-image top and bottom units. Sew the pieces together in each row. Make 30 top and 30 bottom units measuring 2" x 4¼", including seam allowances.

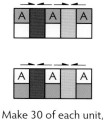

Make 30 of each unit,
2" × 4¼".

4 Referring to the diagram, lay out the following pieces in five rows as shown: one top and one bottom unit from step 3, one orange 1¼" × 4¼" rectangle, one B segment, and one navy 1¼" × 4¼" rectangle. Sew the pieces together in each row. Join the rows. The unit should measure 4¼" × 5¾", including seam allowances. Make 30 units.

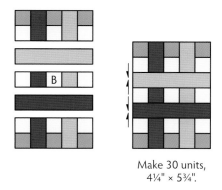

Make 30 units,
4¼" × 5¾".

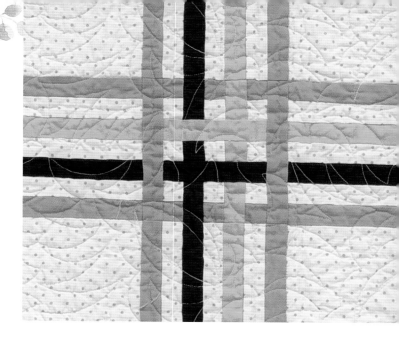

5 Sew green 1¼" × 5¾" rectangles to opposite edges of a step 4 unit to make a block. The block should measure 5¾" square, including seam allowances. Repeat to make 30 blocks.

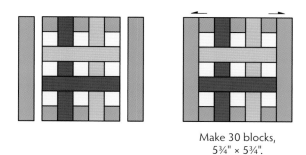

Make 30 blocks,
5¾" × 5¾".

6 Sew together one orange, one navy, two green, and three white 1¼" × 42" strips as shown to make strip set C; be sure to press as shown so that seam allowances will abut, making final quilt assembly easier. Make 10 of strip set C. Crosscut the strip sets into 49 block segments, 5¾" wide, and 22 border segments, 3½" wide.

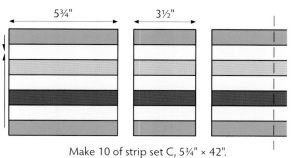

Make 10 of strip set C, 5¾" × 42".
Cut 49 block segments, 5¾" × 5¾".
Cut 22 border segments, 3½" × 5¾".

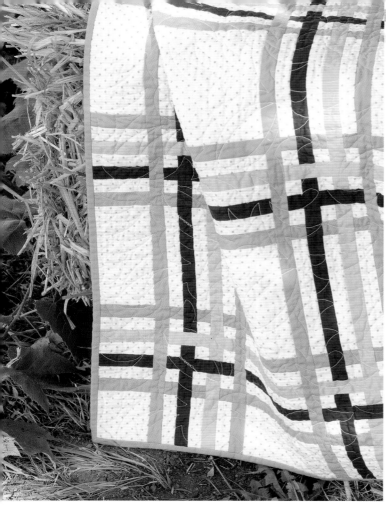

assembling the quilt top

Instead of piecing the blocks and borders separately, I put the entire quilt together in 13 horizontal rows. This leaves less room for error than piecing the side borders first and then attaching them to the quilt center.

1 Lay out two white 3½" squares, five border segments, and four white 3½" × 5¾" rectangles in a row as shown. Be sure block segments are oriented as shown so that the finished quilt will have the woven look of the original. Sew the pieces together to make row 1, which should measure 3½" × 53¾", including seam allowances. Make two of row 1.

Row 1.
Make 2 rows, 3½" × 53¾".

2 Lay out two border segments, five blocks, and four block segments in a row, being sure the pieces are oriented as shown. Sew the pieces together to make row 2, which should measure 5¾" × 53¾", including seam allowances. Make six of row 2.

Row 2.
Make 6 rows, 5¾" × 53¾".

3 Lay out two white 3½" × 5¾" rectangles, five block segments, and four white 5¾" squares in a row, being sure the pieces are oriented as shown. Sew the pieces together to make row 3, which should measure 5¾" × 53¾", including seam allowances. Make five of row 3.

Row 3.
Make 5 rows, 5¾" × 53¾".

4 Referring to the quilt assembly diagram below, lay out the pieced rows and sew them together to complete the quilt top.

finishing the quilt

Find free, detailed finishing instructions online at ShopMartingale.com/HowtoQuilt.

1 Prepare the quilt backing so that it is about 6" larger in both directions than the quilt top.

2 Layer the backing, right side down; the batting; and the quilt top, right side up. Baste the layers together.

3 Hand or machine quilt as desired. The quilt shown is machine quilted with an allover flame design.

4 Using the green 2½"-wide strips, make the binding and attach it to the quilt.

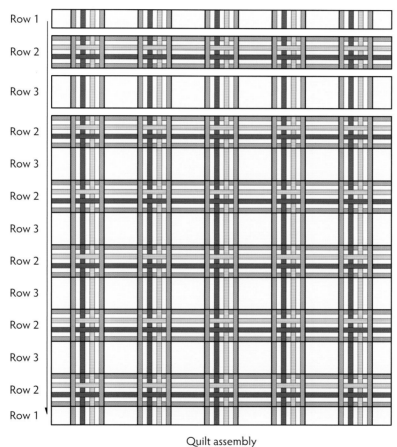

Row 1
Row 2
Row 3
Row 2
Row 3
Row 2
Row 3
Row 2
Row 3
Row 2
Row 3
Row 2
Row 3
Row 2
Row 1

Quilt assembly

Which Hat?

I always keep my fabrics sorted by color and in stacks where I can see them all. At the time I made these hats, I knew the blocks would be little, and I knew that I would want a large variety of gray and black fabrics. So I just cut off a small chunk of each fabric that I loved and started my millinery assembly line. The backgrounds were a fun pile of anything that had a hint of black or gray.

materials

Yardage is based on 42"-wide fabric. Fat quarters are 18" × 21". Fat eighths are 9" × 21".

- 13 fat quarters of assorted light prints for blocks and sashing
- 29 fat eighths or ⅛-yard pieces of assorted black and gray prints (collectively referred to as "dark") for blocks and outer border
- 22 strips, 2½" × 42", of assorted orange prints for outer border
- ⅜ yard of cream print for inner border
- ⅝ yard of mottled dark gray print for binding
- 4⅛ yards of fabric for backing
- 73" × 76" piece of batting
- Template plastic

cutting

All measurements include ¼" seam allowances. Trace triangle patterns A and B on page 50 onto template plastic and cut out on the drawn lines. Trace the templates onto the wrong side of the 3½"-wide strips as specified at right and on page 46, rotating the templates 180° after each cut to make the best use of your fabric. Note that very little waste remains from the light and dark print pieces; be careful when cutting.

From *each* light print fat quarter, refer to the diagram below to cut:

1 strip, 5" × 21" (13 total); crosscut into:
- 1 rectangle, 2½" × 5" (13 total)
- 11 rectangles, 1½" × 5" (143 total)

3 strips, 3½" × 21" (39 total); crosscut into:
- 12 A and 12 A reversed triangles (156 total of *each*)
- 19 rectangles, 1¼" × 3½" (247 total)

1 strip, 1¼" × 21" (13 total); crosscut into 5 rectangles, 1¼" × 3½" (65 total)

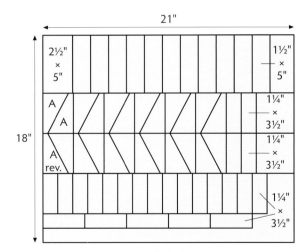

Cutting for light fat quarters

Continued on page 46

Continued from page 44

From *each* dark print, refer to the diagram below to cut:

If using fat eighths:

1 strip, 3½" × 21" (29 total); crosscut into 6 B triangles (174 total; 18 are extra)

3 strips, 1½" × 21" (87 total); crosscut into:
- 6 rectangles, 1½" × 5" (174 total; 18 are extra)
- 12 squares, 1½" × 1½" (348 total; 4 are extra)

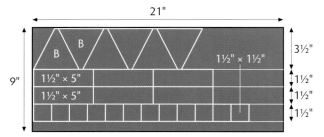

Cutting for dark fat eighths

If using ⅛-yard pieces:

1 strip, 3½" × 14½" (29 total); crosscut into 6 B triangles (174 total; 18 are extra)

2 strips, 1½" × 25½" (58 total); crosscut into:
- 6 rectangles, 1½" × 5" (174 total; 18 are extra)
- 12 squares, 1½" × 1½" (348 total; 4 are extra)

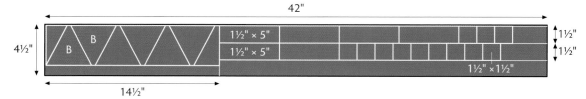

Cutting for dark print ⅛-yard pieces

From *each* orange print strip, cut:

16 squares, 2" × 2" (352 total; 8 are extra)

From the cream print, cut:

4 strips, 1½" × 42"

4 strips, 1¼" × 42"

From the mottled dark gray print, cut:

8 strips, 2½" × 42"

Quilt size: 66½" × 69½"
Block size: 4½" × 4"

making the blocks

Press the seam allowances as indicated by the arrows.

1 Sew a light A triangle to one edge of a dark B triangle; be sure the blunt tip of the B triangle is pointing upward. Press. Add a matching A reversed triangle to the adjacent edge of the dark triangle. Make 156 units that measure 3½" square, including seam allowances.

Make 156 units,
3½" × 3½".

2 Matching the light print, sew light 1¼" × 3½" rectangles to opposite sides of a unit from step 1 to make a hat unit. The unit should measure 5" × 3½", including seam allowances. Make 156 hat units.

Make 156 units,
5" × 3½".

3 Matching the dark print, sew a dark 1½" × 5" rectangle to the bottom edge of a hat unit to make a block. The block should measure 5" × 4½", including seam allowances. Make 156 blocks.

Make 156 blocks,
5" × 4½".

assembling the quilt top

1 Lay out 12 blocks and 11 assorted light 1½" × 5" rectangles in a row as shown, alternating pieces. Sew together to make a block row. Make 13 rows that each measure 5" × 59½", including seam allowances.

Make 13 rows,
5" × 59½".

2 Referring to the quilt assembly diagram, lay out the block rows and light 2½" × 5" sashing rectangles in 13 columns. Arrange the odd-numbered columns with a light 2½" × 5" sashing rectangle on the bottom and the even-numbered columns with a light 2½" × 5" sashing rectangle on the top. Join the columns. The quilt top should measure 59" × 61½", including seam allowances.

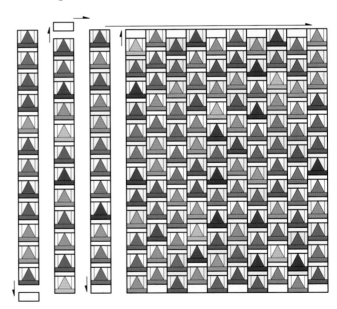

Quilt assembly

making the border units

1 Use a pencil to mark a diagonal line on the wrong side of each dark 1½" square.

2 Align a marked square, right sides together, on one corner of an orange 2" square as shown. Sew on the drawn line. Trim the seam allowances to ¼". Make four matching units, pressing the seam allowances on two units toward the orange and on two units toward the dark. Repeat to make 86 sets of four matching units (172 pressed toward the orange and 172 pressed toward the dark).

Make 172 of each unit,
2" × 2".

3 Lay out four matching units from step 2 in pairs; to reduce bulk, alternate the units so that seam allowances are pressed in opposite directions. Sew together the units in each pair. Join the pairs to make a border unit that measures 3½" square, including seam allowances. Make 86 border units.

Make 86 units,
3½" × 3½".

adding the borders

1 Sew together 21 border units to make a strip that measures 3½" × 63½", including seam allowances. Make two for the side outer borders.

Make 2 borders,
3½" × 63½".

2 Sew together 22 border units to make a strip that measures 3½" × 66½", including seam allowances. Make two for the top and bottom outer borders.

Make 2 borders,
3½" × 66½".

3 Join the cream 1¼" × 42" strips end to end and press the seam allowances open. Cut the pieced strip into two 61½"-long strips for the side inner borders. Sew the side inner-border strips to opposite edges of the quilt top.

4 Join the cream 1½" × 42" strips end to end and press the seam allowances open. Cut the pieced strip into two 60½"-long strips. Sew these strips to the top and bottom of the quilt; the quilt top should measure 60½" × 63½", including seam allowances.

5 Sew the pieced side outer-border strips to opposite edges of the quilt top. Add the pieced top and bottom outer-border strips to the remaining edges to complete the quilt top.

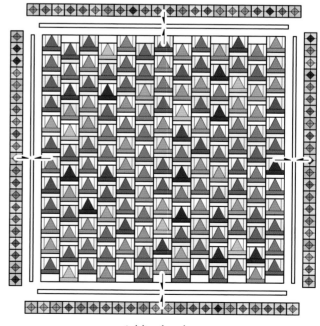

Adding borders

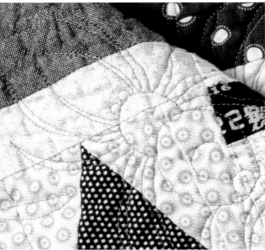

finishing the quilt

Find free, detailed finishing instructions online at ShopMartingale.com/HowtoQuilt.

1 Prepare the quilt backing so that it is about 6" larger in both directions than the quilt top.

2 Layer the backing, right side down; the batting; and the quilt top, right side up. Baste the layers together.

3 Hand or machine quilt as desired. The quilt shown is machine quilted with an allover spider design.

4 Using the mottled dark gray 2½"-wide strips, make the binding and attach it to the quilt.

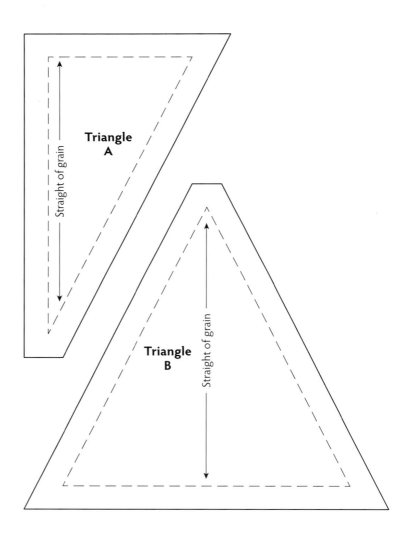

Triangle A

Straight of grain

Triangle B

Straight of grain

Cocoa Grande

In my experience shopping for vintage baby quilts, they are not as easy to find as other antique quilts. I do hope that is because they have been used and loved and continue to be passed down through the generations. But an antique baby quilt is exactly where I got the idea for this biggie-size bundle of fun. My baby version is faded and worn, which is the very reason why I wanted to make a biggie version to snuggle in during the cold winter months. Relying on my stash of shirting prints as backgrounds, and tossing in tan, brown, and some eggplant, I think I was able to capture the feel of the mini sweetness that I was after.

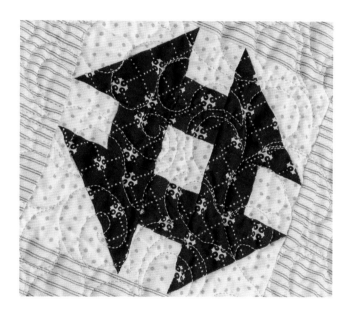

cutting

All measurements include ¼" seam allowances. To achieve the look of a continuous stripe in the setting squares and triangles, refer to the cutting diagram on page 53 when cutting the light blue stripe.

From *each* medium or dark print, cut:

2 strips, 2⅞" × 21" (40 total); crosscut into:

- 8 squares, 2⅞" × 2⅞" (160 total). Cut each square in half diagonally to yield 16 triangles (320 total).
- 3 squares, 1½" × 1½" (60 total)

1 strip, 1½" × 21" (20 total); crosscut into 13 squares, 1½" × 1½" (260 total)

From *each* shirting print, cut:

2 strips, 2⅞" × 21" (40 total); crosscut into:

- 8 squares, 2⅞" × 2⅞" (160 total). Cut each square in half diagonally to yield 16 triangles (320 total).
- 7 squares, 1½" × 1½" (140 total)

1 strip, 1½" × 21" (20 total); crosscut into 13 squares, 1½" × 1½" (260 total)

Continued on page 53

materials

Yardage is based on 42"-wide fabric. Fat eighths are 9" × 21".

- 20 fat eighths of assorted medium and dark prints (3 eggplant, 8 brown, 9 tan) for blocks
- 20 fat eighths of assorted shirting prints for blocks
- 2⅓ yards of light blue stripe for setting squares and triangles
- 1⅝ yards of light brown print for border and binding
- 4⅞ yards of fabric for backing
- 71" × 86" piece of batting

Continued from page 51

From the light blue stripe, refer to the diagrams below to cut:

3 strips, 6½" × 42"; crosscut into:

- 7 squares, 6½" × 6½". Cut each square in half diagonally from upper left to lower right to make 14 top/bottom setting triangles.
- 9 squares, 6½" × 6½". Cut each square in half diagonally from lower left to upper right to make 18 left/right setting triangles.

9 strips, 5½" × 42"; crosscut into 63 squares, 5½" × 5½"

2 squares, 5" × 5", cut on the *bias*. Cut each square in half diagonally as shown below to yield 4 corner triangles.

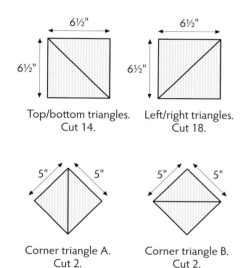

Top/bottom triangles. Cut 14.

Left/right triangles. Cut 18.

Corner triangle A. Cut 2.

Corner triangle B. Cut 2.

From the light brown print, cut:

7 strips, 4½" × 42"

8 strips, 2½" × 42"

making the blocks

Press the seam allowances as indicated by the arrows.

1 Sew together a medium or dark triangle and a shirting triangle to make a half-square-triangle unit. The unit should measure 2½" square, including seam allowances. Make four matching half-square-triangle units.

Make 4 units, 2½" × 2½".

2 Using the same prints as in step 1, sew together a medium or dark 1½" square and a shirting 1½" square to make a side unit. The unit should measure 1½" × 2½", including seam allowances. Make four matching side units.

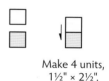

Make 4 units, 1½" × 2½".

3 Lay out the half-square-triangle units, side units, and one matching shirting 1½" square in three rows as shown. Sew the pieces together in each row. Join the rows to make a Churn Dash block that measures 5½" square, including seam allowances. Repeat to make 80 Churn Dash blocks.

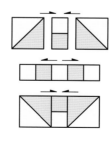 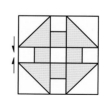

Make 80 blocks, 5½" × 5½".

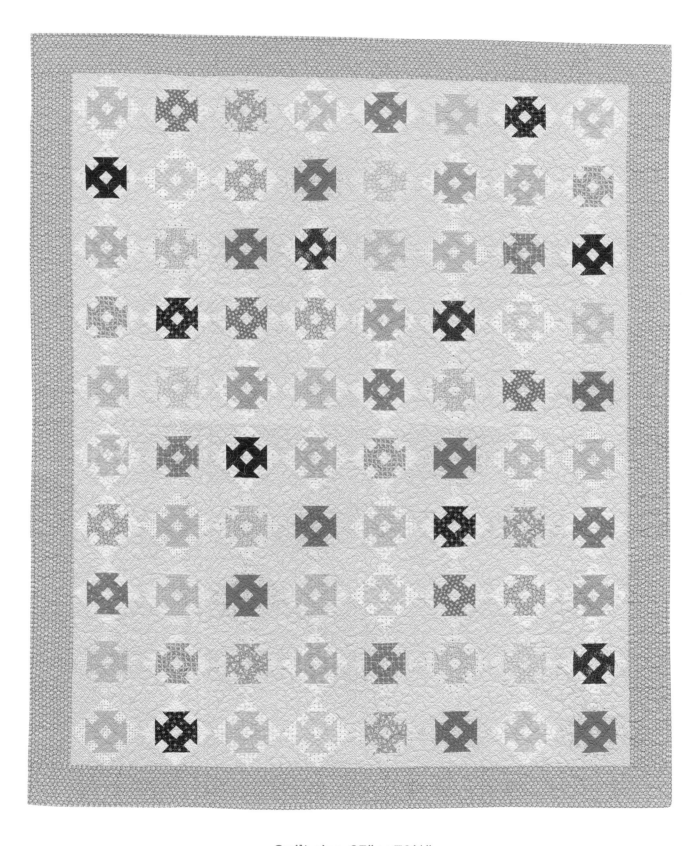

Quilt size: 65" × 79¼"
Block size: 5" × 5"

assembling the quilt top

1 Referring to the quilt assembly diagram below, lay out the blocks, light blue stripe 5½" setting squares, and light blue stripe side and corner triangles in diagonal rows. Pay attention to the stripe orientation when positioning the striped setting pieces so that all stripes run in the same direction. Note that the setting triangles are oversized and will be trimmed after assembly. Sew together the blocks, squares, and triangles in each diagonal row. The outside edges of the setting triangles are on the bias, so be careful not to stretch them out of shape when sewing.

2 Join the rows and add the corner triangles. Carefully trim the excess from the side and corner triangles, ¼" beyond the points of the blocks. The quilt top should measure 57" × 71¼", including seam allowances.

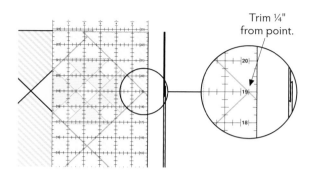

Trim ¼" from point.

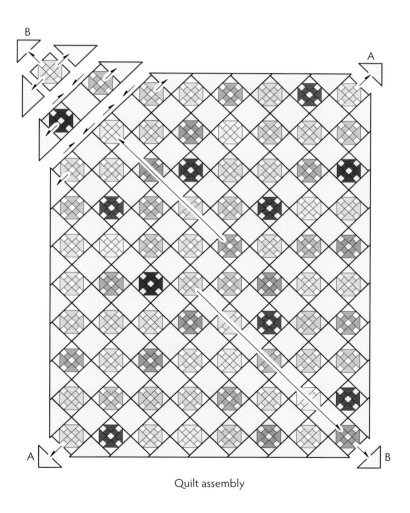

Quilt assembly

adding the border

1 Join the light brown print 4½" × 42" strips end to end and press the seam allowances open. Trim the pieced strip into two 71¼"-long strips and two 65"-long strips.

2 Sew the long border strips to opposite edges of the quilt top. Add the short border strips to the remaining edges to complete the quilt top.

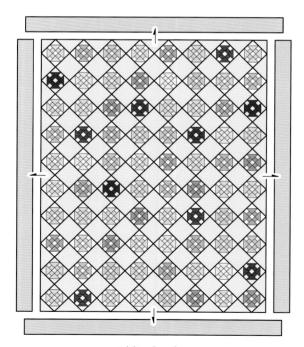

Adding borders

finishing the quilt

Find free, detailed finishing instructions online at ShopMartingale.com/HowtoQuilt.

1 Prepare the quilt backing so that it is about 6" larger in both directions than the quilt top.

2 Layer the backing, right side down; the batting; and the quilt top, right side up. Baste the layers together.

3 Hand or machine quilt as desired. The quilt shown is machine quilted with an allover meandering feather design.

4 Using the light brown print 2½"-wide strips, make the binding and attach it to the quilt.

Sweater Weather

My favorite part about laundry day is actually the sock matching. I find it very satisfying when I get to the bottom of the basket and there isn't a lone sock left. Well, this quilt idea came to me straight from the laundry basket. Yes, argyle socks were my inspiration.

materials

Yardage is based on 42"-wide fabric.

- 3¾ yards of ivory solid for blocks, setting triangles, inner and outer borders, and binding
- 9 strips, 2½" × 42", of assorted gray prints for blocks
- 8 strips, 2½" × 42", of assorted aqua prints for blocks
- ⅝ yard of gray solid for blocks and middle border
- ⅓ yard of aqua solid for blocks
- 3½ yards of fabric for backing
- 63" × 63" piece of batting

cutting

All measurements include ¼" seam allowances.

From the ivory solid, cut:

2 strips, 8½" × 42"; crosscut into 6 squares, 8½" × 8½". Cut each square into quarters diagonally to yield 24 side triangles.

6 strips, 6" × 42"; crosscut into 36 squares, 6" × 6". Cut each square into quarters diagonally to yield 144 block triangles.

1 strip, 5" × 42"; crosscut into 2 squares, 5" × 5". Cut each square in half diagonally to yield 4 corner triangles.

13 strips, 2½" × 42"

5 strips, 2" × 42"

16 strips, 1¼" × 42"; crosscut into:
- 17 strips, 1¼" × 21"
- 49 strips, 1¼" × 5¼"

From *each* gray print and aqua print strip, cut:

2 strips, 2½" × 21

From the gray solid, cut:

4 strips, 2" × 42"; crosscut into 72 squares, 2" × 2"

6 strips, 1½" × 42"

From the aqua solid, cut:

4 strips, 2" × 42"; crosscut into 72 squares, 2" × 2"

making block A

Press the seam allowances as indicated by the arrows.

1 Sew together two matching gray print 2½" × 21" strips and one ivory 1¼" × 21" strip to make a gray strip set. Make nine gray strip sets and crosscut each one into six segments, 2½" wide (54 segments total).

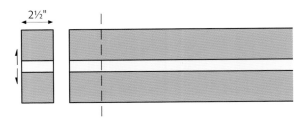

Make 9 strip sets, 5¼" × 21".
Cut 54 segments, 2½" × 5¼".

2 Sew together two matching aqua print 2½" × 21" strips and one ivory 1¼" × 21" strip to make an aqua strip set. Make eight aqua strip sets and crosscut each one into six segments, 2½" wide (48 segments total).

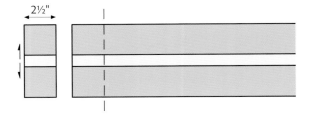

Make 8 strip sets, 5¼" × 21".
Cut 48 segments, 2½" × 5¼".

3 Sew together two matching gray segments and one ivory 1¼" × 5¼" strip as shown to make a gray A block. The block should measure 5¼" square, including seam allowances. Repeat to make 25 gray A blocks. (You will have 4 extra gray segments.)

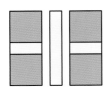 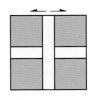

Make 25 A blocks,
5¼" × 5¼".

4 Sew together two matching aqua segments and one ivory 1¼" × 5¼" strip as shown to make an aqua A block. The block should be 5¼" square, including seam allowances. Repeat to make 24 aqua A blocks.

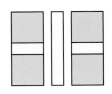

Make 24 A blocks,
5¼" × 5¼".

making block B

1 Use a pencil to mark a diagonal line on the wrong side of each gray solid and aqua solid 2" square.

2 Position a marked gray square, right side down, on the right-angle corner of an ivory block triangle. Sew on the drawn line. Trim the seam allowances to ¼" and press the resulting triangle open. Make 72 units, pressing the seam allowances on 36 triangles toward the gray and on 36 toward the ivory.

Make 36 of each unit.

3 Using the marked aqua squares and the remaining ivory block triangles, repeat step 2 to make 72 units, pressing the seam allowances on 36 units toward the aqua and on 36 toward the ivory.

Make 36 of each unit.

Quilt size: 56½" × 56½"
Block size: 4¾" × 4¾"

4 Arrange four units from step 2 in pairs; to reduce bulk, use two units pressed in each direction and alternate them when laying them out so that seam allowances are pressed in opposite directions. Sew together the units in each pair. Join the pairs to make a gray block B measuring 5¼" square, including seam allowances. Make 18 gray B blocks.

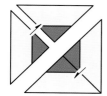

Make 18 B blocks,
5¼" × 5¼".

5 Using the units from step 3, repeat step 4 to make 18 aqua B blocks.

Make 18 B blocks,
5¼" × 5¼".

assembling the quilt top

1 Referring to the quilt assembly diagram below, lay out blocks A and B and the ivory side and corner triangles in diagonal rows. Alternate the A and B blocks in each diagonal row and be sure the blocks in odd rows are gray and the blocks in even rows are aqua. Also note that the setting triangles are oversized and will be trimmed after assembly. Sew together the blocks and triangles in each diagonal row.

2 Join the rows and add the corner triangles. Carefully trim the excess from the side and corner triangles, ¼" beyond the points of the blocks. The quilt top should measure 47½" square, including seam allowances.

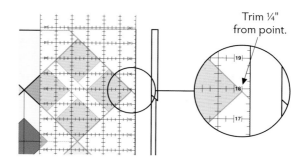

Trim ¼"
from point.

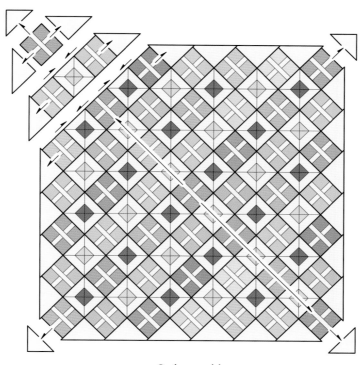

Quilt assembly

adding the borders

1 For the inner border, join the ivory solid 2" × 42" strips end to end and press the seam allowances open. Cut the pieced strip into two 50½"-long strips and two 47½"-long strips. Sew the short strips to opposite edges of the quilt top. Add the long strips to the remaining edges. The quilt top should now measure 50½" square, including seam allowances.

2 For the middle border, join the gray solid 1½" × 42" strips end to end and press the seam allowances open. Cut the pieced strip into two 52½"-long strips and two 50½"-long strips. Sew the short strips to opposite edges of the quilt top. Add the long strips to the remaining edges. The quilt top should now measure 52½" square, including seam allowances.

Susan says . . .

This is a great project to have cut out and ready for a sewing retreat (or for your own personal uninterrupted sewing time). I like it for retreats because it allows you to do repetitive sewing without much thinking—you won't have to worry about getting pieces mixed up if you're talking while sewing! When all of your units are sewn together, head off to the ironing board and press them all at once during gab time with fellow retreaters.

3 For the outer border, join six of the ivory solid 2½" × 42" strips end to end and press the seam allowances open. Cut the pieced strip into two 56½"-long strips and two 52½"-long strips. Sew the short strips to opposite edges of the quilt top. Add the long strips to the remaining edges to complete the quilt top.

finishing the quilt

Find free, detailed finishing instructions online at ShopMartingale.com/HowtoQuilt.

1 Prepare the quilt backing so that it is about 6" larger in both directions than the quilt top.

2 Layer the backing, right side down; the batting; and the quilt top, right side up. Baste the layers together.

3 Hand or machine quilt as desired. The quilt shown is machine quilted with a geometric design of squares, circles, and straight lines in the quilt center. The three borders are treated as one and stitched with a zigzag design of circles and a narrow wave. The remaining portions of the borders are filled with parallel straight lines.

4 Using the remaining ivory solid 2½"-wide strips, make the binding and attach it to the quilt.

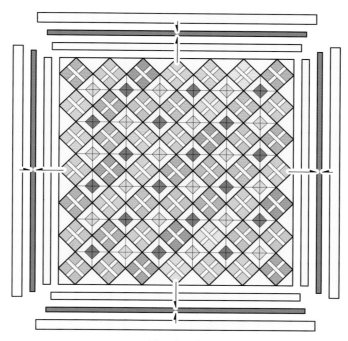

Adding borders

About the Author

Knowing only that she wanted to feature embroidery and Nine Patch blocks, Susan Ache taught herself to make her first quilt. Quiltmaking opened up a new world to this mom of five now-grown children. She turned many hours of reading about quiltmaking into a lifelong passion for creating beautiful quilts.

Susan finds color inspiration in her native Florida surroundings. She's always searching for new and fun ways to show off as many colors as she can in a quilt. Most of her quilts are a creative impulse inspired by a trip to the garden center, a photograph in a magazine, or a few paint color swatches. She never sees just the quilt—she sees the room where the quilt belongs.

Working in a quilt store for years helped cultivate Susan's love of color and fabric. Visit Susan on Pinterest and Instagram as @yardgrl60.